H.G. Wells Investigates
The Tragedy of Colour
In America

H.G. Wells Investigates
The Tragedy Of Colour
In America

Poems by

Alexander Payne Morgan

© 2019 Alexander Payne Morgan. All rights reserved.
This material may not be reproduced in any form, published,
reprinted, recorded, performed, broadcast,
rewritten or redistributed without
the explicit permission of Alexander Payne Morgan.
All such actions are strictly prohibited by law.

Cover design: Shay Culligan
Cover photograph of H.G. Wells: photographer unknown,
possibly Elliott & Fry Studio, circa 1901

ISBN: 978-1-950462-18-6

Kelsay Books Inc.

kelsaybooks.com

502 S 1040 E, A119
American Fork, Utah 84003

To
H.G. Wells, Booker T. Washington,
and all the many others
who have recognized and fought
the insanity of racism.

Acknowledgments

Grateful acknowledgment is made to the editors of the following journals where these poems first appeared:

Bayou Magazine: "The Slave Owner's Daughter Makes Soap"
The Courtship of Winds: "H. G. Wells Investigates the Tragedy of Colour in America" and "Mouse in a Trap by Its Tail"
Crack the Spine: "The Slave Owner's Daughter Pays A Condolence Call" and "The Help"
The Dead Mule School of Southern Literature: "Massie School Still Stands on Gordon Street" (in a slightly different version), "A Sandspur," "Sorry, I've Got to Go," and "My House Has Probably Fallen In by Now"
The Evening Street Review: "Bistro Savannah," "Bus Station Prayer," and "Persistence"
The MacGuffin: "Lucky to Have a Job" and "Ulysses: The Thinker"

"A Sandspur," "Sorry, I've Got to Go," and "The Slave Owner's Daughter Makes Soap" also appeared in my chapbook *Loneliness Among Primates (Kelsay Books, 2018).*

"Ulysses: The Thinker" was an Honorable Mention in the 2013 National Poet Hunt contest judged by Philip Levine.
"The Slave Owner's Daughter Makes Soap" was awarded the 2016 Kay Murphy Prize for Poetry by *Bayou Magazine.*

I greatly appreciate the Detroit-area poetry workshops that have given me useful feedback and encouragement over many years. Thanks to the workshop leaders—Mary Jo Firth Gillett, Mary Ann Wehler, Bethany Schryburt, Lucinda Sabino, and Joy Gaines-Friedler—and to the many participants.

Thanks especially to poets Diane DeCillis, Nadia Ibrashi, Ken Meisel, Nancy Owen Nelson, Dwight Stackhouse, and David Strong, for invaluable support and criticism.

Joy Gaines-Friedler has been important to me in many ways. No mere cataloguing would be adequate. Thank you, Joy.

I want to acknowledge everybody who contributes to the amazing Detroit literary community; in particular, John D. Lamb and M.L. Liebler for making Springfed Arts and the Detroit Writers' Guild such important parts of that community. We're all in this together.

Sands Hall worked with me on my poem "Bistro Savannah" while I was at the Squaw Valley Community of Writers in 2013. Her wonderful sense of humor gave me the courage to find my own.

The Vermont College of Fine Arts poetry-manuscript workshop (summer, 2017) was so helpful and supportive. I want to acknowledge the generous spirit of workshop leader, Matthew Dickman, and my fellow workshop participants.

Thank you Russell Thorburn for pushing me to say more about Ulee, who really was the custodian at Valdosta High School when I was a student there, and for urging me to give the inventor of the time machine his due.

I'm proud to share my life with Janice, Abraham, and Julia. I love you.

Dear Janice, you are so smart, skillful, diplomatic, and generous; I'm lucky to have you as my partner.

Contents

Ulysses: The Thinker	11
The Slave Owner's Daughter Makes Soap	12
The Slave Owner's Daughter Pays a Condolence Call	14
The Help	16
Pep Rally	17
Facilities Not Marked "Colored" Are White Only	18
Worth Doing Right	19
Confederates	20
Bus Station Prayer	22
Sorry, I've Got to Go	23
Fighting	25
Bistro Savannah	29
Lucky to Have a Job	31
Colored Waitress	32
My House Has Probably Fallen In by Now	33
The Valdosta Times Runs Its First Ever "Negro News"	35
Persistence	36
Massie School Still Stands on Gordon Street	39
For a Few Minutes	41
A Sandspur	42
Analysis of Voting Patterns in the U.S. Senate	43
H.G. Wells Investigates the Tragedy of Colour in America	44
Mouse in a Trap by Its Tail	45
Note: H.G. Wells in America	49

Ulysses: The Thinker

Valdosta, Georgia, 1960

Ulee is just the Black janitor
who's swept the halls of Valdosta High School
since before forever
takes his time, observes his White work
situation with slow eyes, allows
the days to pass, likes his indoor job
where the Klan
the Cyclops, the sheriff
won't grin and question.

The yearbook photographer, Robert
poses Ulee as Rodin's "The Thinker" sitting
hand on chin, elbow on knee. Robert
giggling.

Ulee poses, doesn't object, holding still
maintains a tense forbearance, thinks
about the little rented house he
his wife and children might be turned out of
if he objects, thinks
how he gives his wife money
for food and doesn't tell her anything, thinks
how his children run to greet him
when he gets off the bus
and hug him and call him "sir," because
he's taught them something of respect, thinks
when he's cleaning up after the White people's children
he can't afford to object to anything.

Yet, he thinks
too, of one day when he might choose
to string his bow.

The Slave Owner's Daughter Makes Soap

Savannah, 1950

Slaves were worth more than railroad investment, banks and factories nationwide combined in 1860.
                  Corey Brooks, York College Professor of History

I see with five-year-old eyes:
    a wood fire under a cauldron,
    a red round box of lye powder,
    old tin cans filled with bacon fat.

Granny's daddy's slaves used to do this work,
but they got freed
before my granny got born,
she the seventh White daughter
of a White gentleman, bitter
how he got robbed of his property.

Granny jabs her broomstick with two hands.
Her loose hair sprays as she
works the mash,
grips the sandy dirt bare-toed,
strains out her neck,
forces the soap hard. Then
she cuts the remnant
scum into bite-sized squares.

I say:
    Are those squares candy?

Mommy explodes like blood from a whipping:
    Don't touch that stuff.
    It'll rot your fingers off,
    eat your tongue gone,
    burn your eyes
    to black pools of pus.

Granny chuckles:
> *Little boy,*
> *other side Savannah,*
> *ate some lye soap once.*
> *Burned his throat right out,*
> *had to go round with blue strings*
> *tied out his nose.*

Granny loves her terrible stories:
> *a gasoline cigar lighter exploded, burned her uncle,*
> > *burned his face right off;*
> *lady next door dusting her new electric lamp,*
> > *unplugged, but it electrocuted her anyway;*
> *little paperboy crashed his bicycle, his head*
> > *wedged in a culvert,*
> > *died when they tried to pry him free.*

Her stories stick like scum
in my brain for decades,
for decades until I can realize
the bitter glee of her father,
her father's ferocious disbelief as his world inverted.

Mommy sulks,
while Granny stores the soap in her wood crate,
a rough pine box,
the kind oranges come in.

She picks up and puts down
the nasty little soap squares bare-handed.
Lost in the rhythm of long practice,
she doesn't give a spit how much they burn.

The Slave Owner's Daughter Pays a Condolence Call

Savannah, 1953

Eight-year-old me with my ancient granny knocking.
Little Black girl greets us at the door.

"White Lady come to see you," she calls out over her thin
    shoulder.

I never knew I was White.

Hannah comes,
equally ancient, riverbank wrinkles
Tybee-cloud hair
whose deceased daughter tended my granny,
helped her scrub and cook and clean.

Hannah welcomes her unexpected
dowager, my grandmother
powdered skin, ash-cast hair,
quivers on my arm,
settles in the room's best chair.

Hannah takes up a cane-bottomed seat,
but I have to stand, pinned in place
by Granny's grip.

These elders talk and nod and talk.
I would so rather go and play.

With an owner's unselfconscious ease,
my Grandmother weaves
condolence, compliment, reminiscence.

"Weren't things so much simpler when we were girls?"
Hannah nods and smiles, coughs, chokes,
recovers.

Hand-stitched angel dolls
Negro and Caucasian mixed
peer down from shelf and mantel
stand behind glass-fronted cases
line the floor like heaven's breadline.

Even I know these angels aren't happy birds.
They weave their own self threads, hum their
own self tunes, hate
not having teeth.

Little Black girl stands out the front foyer,
looks in at me, smiles, but we can't play.

The Help

Georgiana used ghosts to help her with household tasks. She'd spoken ghost since childhood, which was a great aid in directing them to the simple jobs their incorporeal nature allowed.

The ghosts were particularly good at rousting tarantulas, which the old houses in Savannah tended to be inordinately infested with. Georgiana tolerated ghosts but couldn't bear spiders. These dangerous and disgusting pests scampered off the fruit boats from South America, which made regular stops at Savannah Harbor.

Inevitably, Georgiana's bragging about her "help" raised the suspicions of the federal authorities. Finally, her house was raided by those rude Immigration and Customs Enforcement people. They couldn't catch the ghosts, who just stood around looking sad and translucent, but the ICE agents did succeed in breaking all of Georgiana's ceramic cows, a quite valuable collection of considerable sentimental significance.

Pep Rally

Valdosta, Georgia, 1959

First day of high school in a new town.

History teacher yells:
"Pep rally out back. Go. Everybody."
Follow the crowd. One more first-day confusion.
What's a pep rally? I don't dare ask.

We shout: "We're gonna win. We're gonna win."
How do we know? I wonder, but no time for thinking.
"Push 'em back. Push 'em back. Way back."
Push who where? but I have to stop trying to make sense.

"Hit 'em again. Hit 'em again. Harder. Harder,"
and suddenly I feel it, the crowd becomes

a mob

like Uncle Parker told me:

In this town, just
forty-one years before,
the lynching party
Mary Turner burned
alive, ripped open
so her unborn child
could be stamped dead
by a volunteer from the crowd.

Maybe it was that history teacher.

Maybe he trailed
bloody ashes the next day
when he walked into class.

Facilities Not Marked "Colored" Are White Only

Valdosta, Georgia, 1962

the little paperboy
risked his life by risking a pee

the men's room sign
omitted any qualifying adjective

the boy went in
but White men used that room

one unleashed himself
upon the boy

White only gave the man his license
White solidarity his immunity

but what White childhood
his eagerness?

my mother pleaded the
separate but equal apology
with passionate abstractions

never knew
never wanted to know
about the boy

Worth Doing Right

"If it's worth doing, it's worth doing right."

Which sounds okay, but what does it mean?

Mother decided "right" meant "perfect,"
and with housework in mind,
declared the aphorism absurd.

She was also against "doing good."

A man in our town, homeless, picked his meals
from the bins out back the DeSoto Hotel.

Mother scoffed at the fools
who wanted to help him.
"Maybe he likes to eat garbage."

The dispute with her sister, my Aunt Bea,
who argued we should ask the man
if he wanted to share a portion of our table.

Mother was horrified.
You don't *ask* people.
You don't ask what they want, and
they should know not to ask for it.

Asking would destroy
the *rightness,*
like looking into Schrodinger's box
and killing the cat.

Not asking
is always *perfect,*
always

right.

Confederates

Our new government is founded upon ... the great truth that the negro is not equal to the white man; that slavery ... is his natural and normal condition. This, our new government, is the first in the history of the world based upon this great physical, philosophical, and moral truth.
　　　　　From "The Cornerstone Speech" (1861) by Alexander Stephens, Vice President of the Confederacy

1962.
　　　　　　　Henry,
　　　　　　　　　　　　　a Black
boy,
　　　　　　interviews at
　　　　　　　　　　　　the University of Georgia.
The interviewer
　　　　　　doesn't offer
　　　　　　　　　　　　　to shake his hand,
doesn't offer
　　　　　　him
　　　　　　　　　　　　a seat.

Why
　　　　　　you wanna
　　　　　　　　　　　　come
here,
　　　　　　nigga,
　　　　　　　　　　　　where
you
　　　　　　not
　　　　　　　　　　　　wanted?

Henry thinks:
　　　　　　No
　　　　　　　　　　　　way

they gonna
　　　　　　let me

                                    in,
but
            they
                                    do.

When he sits
            in class,
                        everybody
in his row
            gets up.
                        Moves to another.
The first time
            he goes
                        swimming,
they close
            the pool.
                        Drain it.
His windows
            broken
                        every week.
His room
            set on fire
                        twice.
Henry, persistent
            as a lunatic,
                        graduates
from the
            University of
                        Georgia,
just
            like
                        Alexander Stephens.

Bus Station Prayer

Dear God, let us get on with no trouble.
In the bus station, the family huddles,
eyes cast down, father, mother, daughter, son.
They don't know their place, the signs taken down.

In the bus station, the family huddles,
Black family. I almost forgot that part.
They don't know their place, the signs taken down.
Station not segregated anymore.

The Black family, *they* don't forget that part.
As they huddle, they pray they're in their place.
Station not segregated anymore,
but who knows what White traps are in the room now?

They huddle. They whisper. They feel misplaced.
I'm a White kid confused. What do I see?
Something White and dark left trapped in the room now,
what I never saw when the signs were up.

I'm a White kid displaced by what I see—
downcast eyes, father, mother, daughter, son—
what I should have seen when the signs were up.
Dear God, let us get on with no trouble.

Sorry, I've Got to Go

Malo Mori Quam Foedari (I choose death over dishonor)
                                                  Payne Family Motto

The sun hits the wall of the little nest
my new wife has made of our flat
on Bishop Street, and the light angles
across the old pine floor. March wind
flexes the plastic tacked to the windows,
but Heather, wise in the ways of cats,
has curled up in a plank of sun, and sleeps.

I'm holding the just-arrived with no stamp
single-page onionskin government letter.
Despite jokes and rumors, it doesn't say "Greetings."
I'm frozen.

Carol King looks across barefoot from her record cover.
Dylan's head explodes with psychedelic delirium,
a poster we've thumbtacked over our mattress.

Heather yawns and stretches.

We've argued all year about Canada
or prison, the hard *moral* choices,
or that psychiatrist in Boston who'll write
insane diagnoses, or other
convoluted options.
All that hot talk now stilled
by this one cold paper blade.

Somewhere in me, old blood
pumps with martial obligation.
It's so stupid—it's not even the right war—but no
choice. Never had one. This translucent typed order
nullifies evasion.

I know I'll let them take me.

Fighting

One day, a boy, a fellow fourth-grader,
lets me know we are going to fight after school.
Jimmy has red hair, sticks his lip out,
husky body, moon face, cow shit
on his boots. He's in my class,
but I don't know him.

Who is this guy and why
does he want to fight me?
Why fight someone
you've never talked to?
He is confident,
knows what he's doing.
I'm baffled.
My feelings are hurt, cause he doesn't like me.
He's big, wants to hurt more
than my feelings. Why
does he want to hurt me?

The school day ends. I run home.
He follows me
right up to my front door.

I tell my mother, "Somebody wants to fight me."
"Well, then, I guess you'd better fight."
She escorts me back outside.
Jimmy and I face each other
on the sidewalk, his friends on one side, my mother
on the other.

He hits my shoulder. I hit his shoulder.
He hits my shoulder. I hit his shoulder.
We aren't hitting hard.
I'm still confused. What are the rules

for this fighting thing?
Even my mother
understands, but I don't.
Why are we doing this?

Jimmy is mute, intense, inscrutable. I can't
stand it. "Why you wanna fight me?"

"You stuck up. You think you better
than other people."

That's a shock.
                              "No, I don't."

His eyes cloud with uncertainty.
                              "You don't?"

What does he expect me to say? *I'm better
than scum like you.* Maybe we're
                              supposed to come up with nastier
                                               and nastier
insults, and maybe the hitting's
                              supposed to hurt more and more.

There's some justice to his complaint.
I've never noticed him, never said *Hi* or anything.
Not very friendly of me. Maybe
I hurt *his* feelings.

Or maybe he's just a bully, and I'm
just his prey. I don't know.
He's stopped hitting me.
That's progress.

"I don't think
        I'm better than you, and
                I don't want
                      to fight you."
"Well, okay."
He walks away.

Mother's teachable moment:
"Never
run from a fight.
Be a lion,
not a rabbit."

But I would be proud to be
Br'er Rabbit, who eludes
or talks his way free.

No respect
for that.

After this day of the fight, I borrow
the turtle's shell,
pull in my head
and shield who I am from her and all the rest.

An age passes.

I am drafted.
I crawl through the dirt of Fort Dix with my M-16 rifle
and queue up for Vietnam.

Mother is appalled.

She writes me long tear-stained cursive letters
on fine pink stationary,
soft sentiments of reassurance:
                      "Everything will be okay."

I really am surprised.

I thought she'd be elated,
                her son
                          fighting.

Bistro Savannah

I order the grits and shrimp and get
a prank on my plate.
It has to be.

A tiny mound of yellow grits
with four miniscule shrimp arranged in a wheel
and three bold diagonals of asparagus,
I suppose to impress me with their "color" and "drama."

I'm not immune to the charms of culinary flair, but
what kind of *Savannah* meal is this?

Start with magnitude:
forty makes more sense than four.
Don't peel them and—
it being only civil to let a creature see its fate—
leave the heads on, too.

The shrimp should be served in a bucket,
ready to fight back when nabbed,
and we need a hole in the middle of the table to receive
the inedible portions of the corpses.

Those grits should start out white
in a bowl of sufficient capacity,
at least a quart.
Butter on the side, cheese appreciated.

Who ordered this chardonnay wine?
How about some old-fashioned sweet tea,
kissed with mint, cradled in crushed ice,
reinforced discreetly with bourbon,
like Mother's basic summer-evening libation?

No guest should rise from a Southern table
fit for anything but staggering off to slumber.

Leaving hungry,
offended,
I have to uncover the roots of this gastronomic mendacity.
I arrange a discreet moment with one of the waitstaff.
I knew it!
The owner's from Ohio.

Lucky to Have a Job

Georgia Governor Says Prison Parolees Can Replace Migrant Farm Workers
                The Atlanta Journal-Constitution, June 14, 2011

Sky's pale orange, and Farmer Wilson's here
to pick us over. He wipe his nose. He tall as a sunflower
stalk, face pale as a fresh-sawed pine plank.

We stand patient country mules,
waiting, stirring up
red-clay dust with our
shuffling, hoping
he'll give us a try.

"It's *not* the chain gang," I told Mama, when she
served me her nightmares with my 5 a.m. coffee.
"I'm a genuine free
parolee. I'll bend and pick and sweat
to stay that way."

Mr. Wilson squints: squash
gone to rot up over there,
those zucchini on the other side too ripe, too limp.
We look where he looks. Don't look good.
"Could've really used a crew a couple of weeks ago," he says.
We hope he's not holding *that* against *us*.
"I've got 13 acres of peas down that way." Mr. Wilson points.
He spits. He starts the selection.

Got a friend in line, a boy like me
from Moultrie. He strong, too, like me.
Farmer's going to take him and me.
We laugh at the skinny boys, they pitiful,
they dead squash.

Colored Waitress

Three old White guys walk
into a Waffle House.
They want their food but—strange—
ignore the waitress,

full smiling eager Faye,
look right through Faye. She's
transparent as courtesy.

Then, in a dance so smooth it twirls my brain,
Faye backs out.
Sally sashays in.

They see White Sally, nod, recite their culinary lists,
same breakfast their mamas served
when these three roved barefoot on dirt
Savannah streets, lords of half the population.

Coffee's poured. Eggs with grits are served.
Bacon makes fingers greasy. Sally smiles,
wipes their spills. They whisper among themselves
about the Sand Gnats' disappointing season,
the Federal a-holes mucking with Medicare,
the marsh-grass fires, worse than anyone can remember.

They stand,
look to spit,
remember they can't, toss
cash and leave.

My House Has Probably Fallen In by Now

but I doubt the beach is quite yet gone.
I hear the old Tybee road's still okay,
if you drive slow.
They got rid of those rusted "Erector Set" bridges.
No more waiting while some dumb dinky
boat with a high mast
makes the bridge turn sideways
on a stack of pulleys and gears
I would've loved to've fiddled with
when I was eight.

But don't worry about that.
Find Victory Drive and turn left,
or turn right if you're going the other way,
head east toward the ocean.
The Victory was about World War I,
happened over 100 years ago.
We planted magnolias along that drive,
bloom sweet pink, white, and red in February,
gone by March.

But don't worry about that.
Keep going. Oh, stop for crabs in Thunderbolt.
I mean eat crabs, not crabs foaming over the road
or some weird Biblical shit like that.
Eat crabs if you want but then keep driving
over the stacked stone bridges, five of 'em,
won't turn sideways on gears,
five monuments to junked machinery.

Now it *is* time to worry a little.
Along that flat part around the ruins of Fort Pulaski,
it's been merging with the marsh at high tide. Swamped
is what it's being, reclaimed

up from Florida by the alligators and the pythons,
"for behold, I will send serpents."

Those slimy bastards never dared that
when I was a kid, but the oceans,
the oceans are on the rise, oops,
shush that, that's
blasphemy.

Don't worry about that.
You'll get to the beach if you don't flood out.
Beach'll still there
like I told you.
Those condos though.
Those condos are toast.

Don't worry about them.
Drive around south and look west,
hell of a bloody sunset over the sandbar
where my Aunt Bea
used to hang bait for crabs.

The Valdosta Times Runs Its First Ever "Negro News"

1961, Valdosta, Georgia

Ulee smelled the cat before he saw it.

Strung it up so the photographer
could take his picture and pay Ulee
                                    the promised reward.

Ulee's holding no grudge against bobcats,
even if this one did tear up some dog,
or so some White man says, but Mr. G's
reward is more than Ulee makes from a
                                    week of sweeping.

Mr. G wants to run a whole page of
news about Black folks in Valdosta.
Mr. G's been waiting to have something
big to make White folks gawk and grin.
                                    Dead bobcat'll do.

Big picture of the scary beast, Ulee
sheepish standing there in the shot
                                    waiting to be paid.

The rest just church pot lucks, a birth, school games,
out-of-town relatives come visiting.

Persistence

I visit her grave in Bonaventure Cemetery
once a year in April,
my mother's mother,
the slave owner's daughter,
Beatrice on this stone.
We called her Granny.

I held her hand many times,
a hand that held the hand
that blessed the lacerations
to make the fear
to force the labor.

I still smell terror in the Savannah air.

It's as real as the hydrogen sulfide
from the pulpwood processing plant,
used to be just across the river, the plant
whose "rotten egg" stinks
we joked about as children
and breathed.

Granny talked about her daddy in whispers.
We children waited like hungry dogs
for scraps and bites dropped
by mistake in our hearing.
We snatched up the dripping morsels, ran
to gulp them down
before they could be taken back
or forgotten:

He had seven White daughters, my grandmother
    the baby of the seven.
After "the war," they'd had to sweep
        their own veranda; for shame,
he made them do it after dark.
He'd sold his other children.

Like a Dark-Ages monk
copying Lucretius,
I took down Granny's words
without understanding them.

I look now
sixty years later
at Granny's grave.

I walk around Savannah.

Downtown's gentrified:
    bistros
    gift shops
    ghost tours
    the Savannah School of Art and Design
        with students from
            Cincinnati
            Minneapolis
            Newark
            Detroit.

When I was a kid,
Damned Yankees weren't welcome;
now they flow in a flood, but
what were we afraid of?

They don't change us.
We are as we were.

A Black family waits in the bus station
grouped tense on the colored side. Signs
are down, but they
know.

Three old White guys sit and talk,
want to make things great again,
want life easy like before.

At the library, a young White writer
wows us with his eloquent stories,
then repeats the old ones
about "outside agitators"
and "lying liberal journalists,"
assures us "the colored people
have always been treated
just fine."

Massie School Still Stands on Gordon Street

Built in 1856 on the pattern of an ancient Greek temple,
the golden ratio framed in brick
for classic balance and perfect symmetry.

A temple for learning and reason
built by the enslaved
for the sons of honest sons of Englishmen.
But even the glorious Greeks had slaves.
Even Thomas Jefferson could not give up
the warm comfort of his cradle-to-grave
slaves. Some things are just too choice to cede,
like cane sugar, like broadleaf tobacco, like
incest, those fathered by their masters
and later used, as the custom used to be.

Rain darkens the brick in December. Not
just the walls but the sidewalks are brick, even
some Savannah graves are built from bricks,
but who favors graves, save martyred souls,
and who would be so rude to bring *them* up
in civilized congregations?

I had a third-grade girlfriend at Massie School,
Linda Kay. She told the teacher, crying, begging
not to be kept after school, that her mother
whipped her with a garden hose. It took me
fifty years of puzzling to realize she meant
a hose truncheon like those used by interrogators.
The image I had then was of Linda Kay's mother
wielding a long hose, like a circus act:
Amazing 20-foot garden-hose whipping-
the-Linda-Kay extravaganza.

We've all borne our whippings.
Bear the harm.

The bricks of the temple
can align with lunatic lines of logic
as the sun sets and the mortar shimmers
with whatever liquid has been spilt to mix it.

You can still enjoy the classic symmetry.
Massie School still stands on Gordon Street.

For a Few Minutes

you let me capture you
to show you the beautiful radio I made myself,
just odds and ends, junk and stuff come alive.
You, my big brother's friend, a seventh grader.

I showed you the amazing radio I made myself,
me, my big brother's third grade nuisance,
you, my big brother's friend, a seventh grader.
I dragged you off our front porch,

me, my big brother's third grade nuisance.
I was dying to show someone my coiled contraption.
I dragged you inside from the porch
to admire my jumble of cardboard, thumbtacks, wire and stuff.

I had to show someone it worked, my contraption.
You let me show you.
You admired my jumble of cardboard, thumbtacks, wire and stuff.
You suggested I add a cat's whisker detector.

You let me show you.
You listened to my radio.
Next day, you brought me a cat's whisker detector
and helped me wire it in without messing it up.

You listened to my radio.
I was too much the child to think to thank you.
A few years later a truck accident messed you up.
I didn't know what to do when they told me you were dead,

before I could grow up enough to think to thank you.
You, me, just odds and ends, junk and stuff come alive.
I didn't know what to do when they told me you were dead.
Thank you for letting me have you
                    for a few minutes.

A Sandspur

magnified is a rod of spikes.
I know. I rigged the photomicrograph they used
in the Valdosta High School yearbook for years after I fled.
An eccentric icon for a high school,
you might say, but a certain rough humor
was de rigueur in that territory.

Backlighted, it's strangely translucent. The stem
leads upward on a slant. The barbs appear
too rounded at this magnification to penetrate,
but they'll stick fine at their own scale,
as you try to clear your socks
or your brain,
whichever the most compelling penetration.

There was Coach J who liked ripe reddened
boy asses. I hated his grin. He got run
out of town sometime around 1961.
And the thirty-year-tenured Bible-quoting
Miss R who gave girls A's, boys D's,
finally fired, finally, the year before the year
she would have spiked me on her D.

Sandspur sap flows with why complain
when you'll be the one gets the blame.

But like I say, you had to take hold of the humor
as you ended each day picking out the sharp
spine-covered burrs.

Analysis of Voting Patterns in the U.S. Senate

Coach J's paddle:
polished and varnished,
marked with a crude anatomical illustration,
holes drilled like a frame for penetration.

Humor its veneer and camouflage,
boys bend over for the sweating fat man
grinning, expecting grins
submission
pedophilic communion.

A tool to cure empathetic impulses.

Southern politicos—approving pain,
numb about violation—vote their creed:
God wants the weak to feel their shaming.

The coach can't help but tremble in anticipation.
His boys take their swats, their final examination.

H.G. Wells Investigates the Tragedy of Colour in America

USA, 1906

Traveling in ex-Confederate terrain,
the inventor of The Time Machine asks
his White southern hostess to explain:

"How do you see your grandchildren
and the grandchildren of these people living
side by side?"

She goes pale at the very thought
of "side by side," as he anticipates she will.

Her response is fluttering, deflective, shrewd:
"You have to be *one of us* to feel this
question *at all* as it ought to be felt."

The canny Darwinian knows he's posed
an unanswerable paradox.
The cornerstone of these people's faith,
their unalterable binary,
ignores history and biology.

The lady's mother in the hot night deigned
her Big Daddy play his manly game of
genes, but familial plantation love
turned hard when the property ran to debt.

The Englishman pretends to be confused:
"But they're your *kin*."

"And we care for them," she assures him, "as if
they were our very own children."

Mouse in a Trap by Its Tail

The more Negroes who register to vote as Democrats in the south, the sooner the Negrophobe whites will quit the Democrats and become Republicans.
        Kevin Phillips (Nixon's political strategist), NY Times, 1970

Ulee's janitorial day is done, but
Miss R runs up in a pleading panic.
"The cafeteria, Ulee. Please, the kitchen girls,
they'll faint if they see the mess."

Ulee can't say no, but this day,
this day he's promised
to be home to help his son.

Miss R stays in the hall
while Ulee goes to face her horror.

It's nothing
he hasn't seen before.

The snap that should have snapped a neck
caught only that thin body portion, the end, the tail.
And the flailing, the rattling terror to escape
like a chain-gang jumper, dragging,
who's hardly got a chance.

But wanton killing isn't Ulee's way.

A flick of his thumb gives
freedom, but stunned
the mouse waits as if she can't cipher the courtesy
of this happenstance.

Ulee's thinking of other things.

*My boy heading for Atlanta
to help ole Maynard Jackson get his chance.
Thank God our one-eyed sheriff devil
can't patrol past the county line.
Please God, let it be in Atlanta
White people ain't so mean.*

Ulee gives the floored living thing a finger nudge
and feels her heart, tiny, beating.

He plans to walk his boy
to catch the night bus north. Atlanta
and whatever newer world
he's hoping for,
whatever he can find
even if it kills him.

Ulee will clean up here, discard the bloody trap,
tell Miss R all is well.

He gives the mouse another nudge.
"Go on," he says. "Don't be a fool.
Run."

Note: H.G. Wells in America

Early in the 20th century, H.G. Wells traveled to the United States on assignment as a journalist to write a series of articles from an Englishman's perspective on "life in America" for the popular magazine, *Harper's Weekly*. The articles were collected into a book, *The Future in America,* published in 1906. He wrote on a number of topics and interviewed a variety of citizens.

Chapter XII of *The Future in America* is about American racism. Entitled "The Tragedy of Colour," it describes the destructive force of racism in American culture. It also features an interview with the Black educator and leader, Booker T. Washington. In reflecting on his meeting with Washington, Wells notes "the quality of the resolve, the steadfast effort hundreds of black and coloured men are making to-day to live blamelessly, honourably, and patiently, getting for themselves what scraps of refinement, learning, and beauty they may, keeping their hold on a civilization they are grudged and denied."

In my poem with H.G. Wells in the title, "You have to be one of us…" is quoted directly from the first page of Chapter XII. The rest of the poem reflects and paraphrases ideas expounded in that chapter.

About the Author

Alexander Payne Morgan was born in Savannah, Georgia. His chapbook, *Loneliness Among Primates,* was published in 2018 by Kelsay Books. His poems have appeared in *The MacGuffin, Crack The Spine, Dunes Review,* and *The Dead Mule School of Southern Literature,* among others. He was awarded the 2016 Kay Murphy Prize for Poetry by *Bayou Magazine* and the 2016 Detroit Working Writers *MacGuffin* Poetry Prize. He's a member of Detroit Working Writers, Detroit Writers' Guild, Michigan Writers, and the Poetry Society of Michigan. He is a retired industrial mathematician.

www.ingramcontent.com/pod-product-compliance
Lightning Source LLC
Chambersburg PA
CBHW021028090426
42738CB00007B/938